Katie Dicker and Sam Dilkes

WAYLAND

Published in 2014 by Wayland

Copyright © Wayland 20014

Wayland
Hachette Children's Books
338 Euston Road
London NW1 3BH

Wayland Australia
Level 17/207 Kent Street
Sydney, NSW 2000

Managing Editor: Rasha Elsaeed
Produced for Wayland by
White-Thomson Publishing Ltd.
210 High Street,
Lewes BN7 2NH
Editor: Katie Dicker
Designer: Clare Nicholas
Editorial consultant: Daniel Owers
Photographer: Chris Fairclough

British Library Cataloguing in Publication Data
Dicker, Katie
I belong to the Christian faith
1. Christianity - Juvenile literature
I. Title II. Dilkes, Sam
248

ISBN 978 0 7502 8874 3

First published in 2008 by Wayland

Printed in China

Wayland is a division of Hachette Children's Books, an Hachette Livre UK company.

Acknowledgements

The author and publisher would like to thank the following people for their help and participation in this book:
The Dilkes family, Rev Danny Wignall and all at St. Stephen's Church, Shottermill, Surrey

The website addresses (URLs) included in this book were valid at the time of going to press. However, because of the nature of the Internet, it is possible that some addresses may have changed, or sites may have changed or closed down since publication. While the author and publisher regret any inconvenience this may cause the readers, no responsibility for any such changes can be accepted by either the author or the publisher.

Disclaimer

The text in this book is based on the experience of one family. While every effort has been made to offer accurate and clearly expressed information, the author and publisher acknowledge that some explanations may not be relevant to those who practise their faith in a different way.

Contents

My family 4

Going to church 6

Who is Jesus? 8

Communion 10

Sunday school 12

Getting to know God 14

Praying 16

Living a good life 18

Christian festivals 20

Glossary and further information 22

Index 24

My family

Hi, I'm Sam, and this is my family – my mum and dad and my sisters, Hannah and Molly. We're Christians. Today it's Sunday and we're going to **church** in the village.

Mum and Dad don't work on Sundays so we can all spend the day together.

We go to church to **worship** God who created the world. God lives in **heaven**, but he lives inside me too, because God is everywhere.

Our church is very near so we can walk there. The church has a big **steeple** which points to heaven.

Going to church

At church, we sit down and listen to a **sermon** by the **vicar**. He tells us about God and about a man called Jesus. I like the vicar. He knows a lot of things and he makes us laugh.

The vicar wears a white collar. We call it a dog collar. It goes around his neck, but it doesn't have a lead!

We also sing **hymns** and songs to show how much we love God. We sing about all the things in the world God has given us, and we thank God for looking after us.

Sometimes, I go up to the front of the church with my friends to sing songs we have learnt.

Who is Jesus?

God sent Jesus to live on Earth about 2,000 years ago. Jesus taught people about God and how to live a good life. But some people did not like Jesus. They nailed him on a cross to die.

This statue shows Jesus on the cross. It must have been an awful way to die.

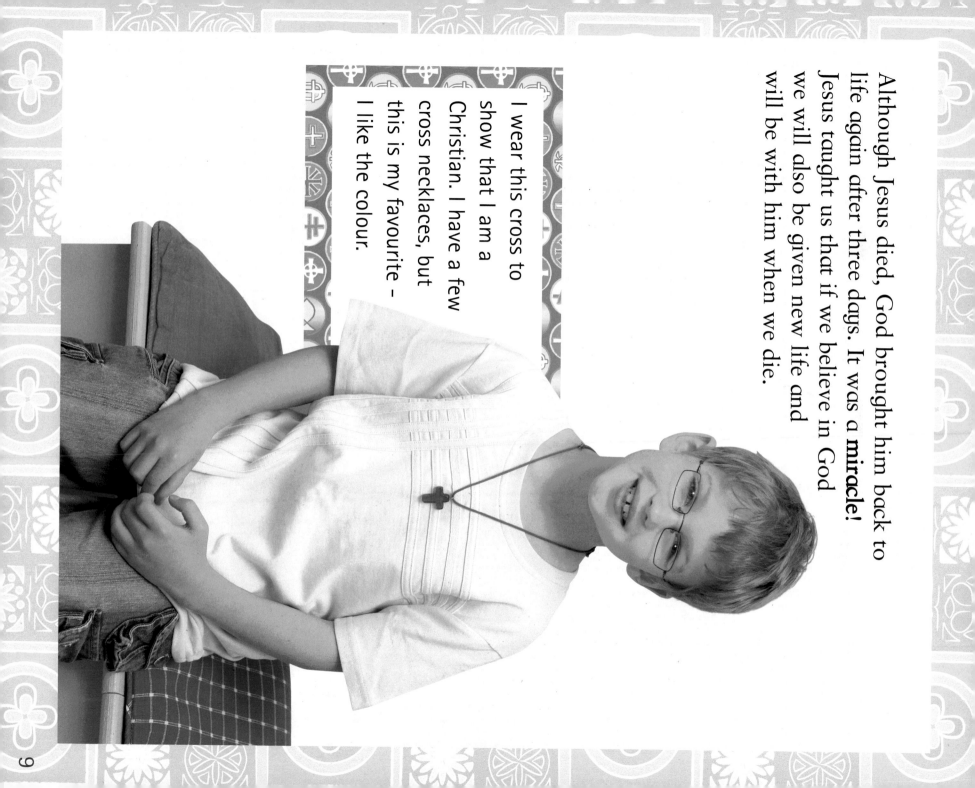

Although Jesus died, God brought him back to life again after three days. It was a **miracle!** Jesus taught us that if we believe in God we will also be given new life and will be with him when we die.

I wear this cross to show that I am a Christian. I have a few cross necklaces, but this is my favourite – I like the colour.

Communion

Before Jesus died he had supper with the **disciples**. Jesus told his friends he would always be with them. There is a big table at the front of the church called the altar. It reminds us of this meal.

The vicar stands behind the altar and holds up some bread and wine.

At church, we go up to the altar to share the bread and wine. We call it **communion**. We eat and drink to remember that although Jesus died, he will always be with us.

The vicar gives me bread and wine. I feel sad when I think that Jesus died for us.

Sunday school

I go to Sunday school with my friends.
We do drama and read **Bible** stories.
Sometimes, we do craft activities.
It's good fun – we learn about
God and about Jesus, but we
have time to play, too.

Today, we're listening
to a story about life in
heaven. We're talking
about what it means
to us.

We learn about the way
Jesus was patient and kind
to other people. If we follow
what Jesus says, we can talk
to him like a friend and do
the things he did to make
other people's lives better.

These words describe
how we can be more like
Jesus. We are putting the
words on a 'tree of life'
so everyone else can
see them.

Getting to know God

We pray to thank God for all the good things in our life. At the end of a **prayer** we say 'Amen'. This means 'I agree' and tells God we really mean what we have said.

Every night, Mum **blesses** me and we say a prayer together. We also ask God to help if we are worried about something.

The Bible is a book full of stories about God and about Jesus. My favourite stories tell us how God made the world, and how Jesus was born in a stable.

I try to read some of the Bible every night, to learn about God and the best way to live.

Praying

Last year, Mum wasn't very well. Lots of people at church prayed for her. Mum is a lot better now. We think that God heard everyone praying and helped to make her well again.

These are some of our friends at church. When Mum was poorly, everyone was thinking about her.

We say prayers for someone we know who is unwell, or for people in the world who are hungry or poor. We pray that their lives will get better and that they will get to know Jesus as a friend, too.

We light candles at church. We do this to pray for other people and to remind us that God is always near.

Living a good life

Jesus taught us to try to be good people. I try to share things with my sisters and to be kind to them. Sometimes it's hard, but I do my best.

My room can get a bit messy. I tidy up and hoover so that Mum doesn't have to.

If we believe in Jesus and behave like him, God will look after us when we die. It's hard to be good all the time, but God gives us a second chance if we say sorry for something we have done wrong.

Dad was cross when I broke this ornament but because he loves me he forgave me when I said sorry.

19

Christian festivals

In December, we celebrate **Christmas**. This is when Jesus was born. We have a big family meal at home and we give each other presents. God gave Jesus as a gift to the world so we like to give presents, too.

At Christmas, we put this nativity scene out at home. It reminds us of all the people who came to see the baby Jesus.

Easter is a very special celebration in the Spring. We remember the time that Jesus came back to life again. We go to church to celebrate and we eat chocolate eggs and hot cross buns!

I help Mum make an Easter garden every year. It's really pretty. We add stones to show where Jesus was buried.

Glossary and further information

Bible – a special book full of stories about God and Jesus.

bless – to ask God to look after something or someone.

church – a building where Christians go to worship God.

communion – the sharing of bread and wine during a Christian service.

disciples – the friends of Jesus who followed his teaching.

heaven – the place where God lives.

hymns – songs that worship God.

miracle – an amazing event.

prayer – a way of talking to God.

sermon – a religious talk.

steeple – a pointed roof.

vicar – a person who leads Christian worship.

worship – to show love and respect to God.

Did you know?

- There are over two billion Christians around the world.

- The word Christianity comes from 'Christ' which means 'someone God has chosen'.

- There are different types of Christians. Some Christians are called Anglicans, Catholics, Baptists or Methodists.

- Sunday is a special day of prayer for Christians because Jesus came back to life on a Sunday.

Activities

1. Arrange to visit a local church. How many symbols of the cross can you find at the church?

2. Do you know any hymns? Try to find the words to a famous hymn. What is it about?

3. Read a story from the Bible and draw a picture to show part of this story.

Books to read

- *A First Look: The Christian Faith* by Lois Rock, Lion Hudson Plc, 2003
- *Special Times with God: Teaching the Basics of Christian Faith to Children* by Anne Faulkner, Barnabas, 2002

Websites

http://www.reonline.org.uk/
This KS1 website explains key features of the Christian religion, with simple text, photographs and audio features.

http://atschool.eduweb.co.uk/carolrb/christianity/
A basic introduction to the Christian religion, with clear text and colourful illustrations.

Organisations

The Church of England
National Church Institutions
Church House
Great Smith Street
London
SW1P 3AZ

Christian festivals

Advent (December)
A time before Christmas when Christians look forward to the birth of Jesus.

Christmas (25 December)
A festival celebrating the birth of Jesus.

Easter (March / April)
A festival to celebrate the fact that when Jesus died, he came back to life again.

Pentecost (May / June)
A celebration of the day that God sent his holy spirit to the disciples to help them to teach other people about God.

Harvest festival (September / October)
A festival to thank God for providing the food that people need to live.

Christian symbols

Cross – a symbol to show the way that Jesus died.

Egg – a symbol of new life.

Fish – many of Jesus' disciples were fishermen and a fish was used as a secret symbol of the church long ago.

Index

A
altar 10, 11

B
Bible 12, 15, 22
blessing 14, 22

C
candle 17
Christmas 20, 23
church 4, 5, 6, 10, 11, 16,
  17, 21, 22
communion 10, 11, 22
cross 8, 9, 23

D
death 8, 9, 11, 19
disciples 10, 22

E
Easter 21, 23

F
family 4, 5, 18, 19, 20
festivals 20, 21, 23
forgiveness 19
friends 7, 12, 13, 16, 17

G
God 5, 6, 7, 8, 9, 12, 14, 15,
  16, 17, 19

H
heaven 5, 12, 22
hymns 7, 22

J
Jesus 6, 8, 9, 10, 11, 12, 13,
  15, 17, 18, 19, 20, 21

K
kindness 13, 18

M
miracle 9, 22

P
prayer 14, 16, 17, 22
presents 20

S
sermon 6, 22
steeple 5, 22
Sunday 4
Sunday school 12
symbols 23

V
vicar 6, 10, 11, 22

W
world 5, 7, 15, 17
worship 5, 22